C000256468

Chainsaw Carving a Bear

By Jamie Doeren

FOX CHAPEL
PUBLISHING

© 2003 by Fox Chapel Publishing Company, Inc.

Chainsaw Carving a Bear is an original work, first published in 2003 by Fox Chapel Publishing Company, Inc. The patterns contained herein are copyrighted by the author. Artists may make up to three photocopies of each individual pattern for personal use. The patterns, themselves, however, are not to be duplicated for resale or distribution under any circumstances. This is a violation of copyright law.

Publisher	Alan Giagnocavo
Book Editor	Ayleen Stellhorn
Cover Design	Jon Deck
Desktop Specialist	Alan Davis

ISBN 978-1-56523-768-1

To learn more about the other great books from Fox Chapel Publishing, or to find a retailer near you, call toll-free 1-800-457-9112 or visit us at **www.FoxChapelPublishing.com**

Note to Authors: we are always looking for talented authors to write new books in our area of woodworking, design, and related crafts. Please send a brief letter describing your idea to Acquisition Editor, 1970 Broad Street, East Petersburg, PA 17520.

Printed in China
First printing
Second printing
Third printing

Because carving wood and other materials inherently includes the risk of injury and damage, this book cannot guarantee that creating the projects in this book is safe for everyone. For this reason, this book is sold without warranties or guarantees of any kind, express or implied, and the publisher and author disclaim any liability for any injuries, losses or damages caused in any way by the content of this book or the reader's use of the tools needed to complete the projects presented here. The publisher and the author urge all carvers to thoroughly review each project and to understand the use of all tools involved before beginning any project.

Table of
Contents

Introduction..1

Chapter One:

Tools and Safety 3

Chapter Two:

Reference Material 7

Chapter Three:

Carving a Cub in a Stump....................................12

Chapter Four:

Carving a Caricature Bear 26

Chapter Five:

Carving a Grizzly Bear 55

Jamie Doeren is a chainsaw carver from Wisconsin. While bears are not his all-time favorite subject to carve with a chainsaw, he grudgingly admits that chainsawed bears are extremely popular among the folks who visit his Wisconsin shop. He is currently working on decorating the interior of a woodland cabin in Wisconsin, which involves carving mantels, staircases and more — all with a chainsaw. You can visit Jamie online at *www.chainsawsculpture. com*.

Introduction

The style and the techniques in this book have been developed through my years of failure and success. Knowing that you must be willing to fail before you can succeed can mean all the difference between ultimate success and repeated failure. Keeping this in mind, remember to refer back to this book when frustration sets in. The only way to get better is to keep at it. Don't worry about fixing your mistakes. Simply finish the carving; then carve another one, correcting the error on this next carving.

For the three carvings in this book, the logical and most practical beginning is to grab a log and rough it out with a chainsaw. The excitement grows as the shape continues to emerge from the log. This sort of carving offers many rewards in terms of physical exercise. As an added plus, chainsaw carving is done out-of-doors, close to nature and in the fresh air.

Through reading and using this book, you will learn techniques to achieve the general recognizable shape of a bear. The objective does not need to be to reproduce every conceivable and minute detail. I do, however, include techniques and instruction within the demonstrations devoted to carving special fea-

A work in progress, this bear will be holding a sign with important information for visitors to the owner's property.

Two bears helping to support this hand-carved bench add interest.

tures such as the eyes, the nose, the claws, the tail and so on. Depending on the style and character of your bear, these features do not need to be used on every bear you carve.

The methods are simple and straight forward. Slight changes in size, pose, behavior, color or overall general character will match the detail correctly to the bear being carved. For example the technique for carving the ear on a black bear might also be applied to a the detail on a grizzly bear's ear.

Each carving project is accompanied by multi-view photos and drawings. Some have important techniques shown with clear, close-up photography to make it easier for the carver to duplicate that particular carving .

Once your first carving is completed, the creative juices will be flowing and other carvings will come in quick succession. Three different patterns are presented in this book, and you can modify them to your needs as you become more comfortable with your chainsaw and more proficient at the art.

As you follow the carvings from the basics of the cub in a stump to the more advanced techniques of chainsaw carving a fierce bear, all you need to succeed is the willingness to try.

The author carved a standing bear with a freshly caught fish in hand as part of a chainsaw demonstration at a local fair.

Chapter One:
Tools & Safety

A safety net is a necessity anytime you will be carving in front of the public—whether it be in a backyard with a family member looking on or at a local fair for many passersby.

When operating a chainsaw, there are a few rules to observe before you should start your saw and begin a chainsaw project.

First, read the safety manual that comes with your saw. All new saws are sold with a safety and operating instruction manual. These manuals will go over all safety issues and the proper operation of your saw.

Second, always choose the right saw for the job and for you. Choosing the right saw is sometimes the most important part of a chainsaw carving project. If you are cutting down a 48" diameter tree, a 16" bar isn't going to go far. But for the purpose of the patterns in this book, you will need relatively small saws.

To choose a saw always look at the size of engine, not the size of bar. The most common mistake I see is people going to a dealer and asking for a 16" saw. That 16" refers to the bar size, not the saw size. The bar just holds the chain; the engine has to turn the chain around the bar. Engine sizes are noted in horse power or cubic centimeters.

Pay close attention to the type of bar you attach to your saw. Every manufacturer has a book that will tell you what length bars their saws can handle. Remember the longer the bar, the more chain there is and the harder the saw has to work. Work with your dealer to pick the saw and bar sizes you will need for your ability. I will recommend a few saws and bars latter.

Third, wear protective clothing, like chaps, boots, gloves, hearing protection, and eye and face protection. Dress accordingly and don't take chances. When I sold saws, countless people told me, "I don't cut very often. I don't need chaps." This statement couldn't be more wrong. Common sense should tell you that the less you cut, the less you know your equipment, which will create a larger margin of error. Even if you work with your chainsaw on a regular basis, don't take shortcuts on the protective clothing. At the risk of sounding like an overprotective parent: Protective gear is a lot less expensive than emergency room visits.

Fourth, make sure the saw is properly maintained and sharp. Poorly main-

Personal safety equipment is a must. Always wear eye protection, ear protection, chaps and steel-toed boots when you carve.

tected from the elements.

You will also need a way to stand up and move large logs and carvings.

Choosing a Chainsaw

Basically, you'll need two types of saws for chainsaw carving: a more powerful saw with a bigger bar to do the roughing out work and a less powerful saw with a smaller bar to do the detail work. You can complete all the projects in this book with one or two saws if you are willing to switch bars and chains several times during a project. This is possible, but I don't recommend it. It is frustrating for beginning carvers and time consuming for any carver.

I will be using four saws throughout the course of this book:

- Husqvarna 246xp with a 12" dime tip bar and 1/4 pitch chain
- Husqvarna 346xp with a 16" bar and 3/8 low pro chain
- Husqvarna 372xp with 20" bar and 3/8 chain
- Husqvarna 394xp with 24" bar and 3/8 chain

You can purchase other saws to match these specs, but I do recommend the tools I use and I'm hard on tools. Shindiawa has a few saws that are smaller, easy to control and can be set up with a 12" carving bar. Echo also makes a smaller saw that handles nicely for beginners. Talk to a knowledge-

tained equipment is dangerous equipment. Keep the chains sharp and your bars true and free of burs. Be sure to use proper bar oil and not some of the more popular but less reliable substitutes. Bar oil is designed for chainsaw bars, and when carving, it pays to use the best quality bar oil available to you. Keep the air filters clean, fresh plug, good starter rope.

Finally, work safe, find a good area in which to work, and keep it clean of debris. Chips and chunks of wood lying at your feet can cause you to trip and fall, so keep them clear of your work area. Use a stump to hold your work and make sure you are carving at a comfortable working height.

Ideally, your back should be straight and you should not have to bend over to make cuts. You may want to have several stumps of varying heights available as you work on bigger or more complex projects.

When you are considering a spot for your work area, be sure that you have shade from the sun and shelter from the rain. Remember, if you want to carve whenever you want to, you need to be proable saw dealer if you plan to match these specs with other saws.

Choosing a Carving Bar

Carving bars come from a couple of different manufactures and private makers. They are made in a few general lengths — 12", 14", 18"—and with several tips — dime, nickel and quarter tips. Other variations and lengths are available, but those I've listed are the most common.

Choosing a Chain

You can run different sized chains on carving bars, but 1/4 pitch is my recommendation. 1/4 pitch is smaller will give you better detail. Never try to run 3/8 low pro or .325 on a dime tip bar because it will burn them up or split the tip. Talk to a knowledgeable saw dealer if you need expert advice on choosing a chain.

A tarp provides important protection from the elements – everything from the heat of the sun to rain.

Finishing a Project

Finishing can be done in a number of ways, the most common of which are burning and painting. I will give some tips here for burning and painting a finished project, but keep in mind that not all processes work in all climates. On the west coast, for example, there are rainy areas and desert areas. Some basic finishing techniques work in both places, however, other techniques work well in one area but not the other. When it comes to finishing, my best advice is talk to the paint experts in the area you live to find out what paints and preservatives work best in your area.

Burning is a process that uses a propane torch to burn, and sometimes even char, the surface of the finished project. The surface is then brushed for a more dramatic effect. This process has some drawbacks: Brushing can get very messy and the burned color can fade from exposure to sunlight. Overall, though, burning is still a very fast and quick way to get a nice finishing job and clean off any "fuzz" left from the saw. Followed by a few coats of varnish, the piece will last a lifetime outside if it is well maintained.

Painting is normally done by sealing the carving, then painting it, then applying a sealer or a varnish the dried paint. Sometimes, if there is a lot of fuzz, you can lightly burn the carving and then seal it for painting. Some paints fade, but the color difference is so slight that it isn't normally noticeable to the passerby. Sign paint, which doesn't fade, is also available, as are pigments to make your own colors. All of these give you a wide range of shades to use. Whatever you choose, take your time. Painting is the one finishing process that can either make a poor carving look great or great carving look poor. Don't be afraid to repaint it if you don't like it.

I personally like to use a wood preservative prior to painting a final project. I don't use a varnish unless a job or customer asks for it.

Chapter Two:
Reference Material

Gathering reference material is an important part of starting any carving project. Chainsaw carving a bear is no exception. On the next several pages, you will find some reference photos for a variety of bears. This section is by no means complete. It is just a sampling to get you started.

Reference material can take a number of forms. Photographs are ideal. You can take your own pictures of animals at a local zoo or wildlife preserve. Magazines and books on wildlife and natural regions are another great source of animal photographs. The Internet, too, is yet another place to find animal pictures. Television shows will give you a good idea of the poses and habitat of your chosen subjects.

Gather reference photos of bears, then study these photos to understand hair flow, posture and attitude. These photos can also be used in the future to sketch out ideas for other bear carvings.

Chapter Three:
Carving a Cub in a Stump

The cub peeking out of a stump is the best form I have found for teaching chainsaw carving. After my students have mastered this project, the rest of the body becomes very easy. Before we get started on this project, you will need the following items.

1. Chaps
2. Safety glasses
3. Hearing protection
4. Steel-toed boots
5. Gloves
6. Chainsaw (approximately 31cc to 55cc)
7. Carving bar (14" to 16" with a 3/8" low profile chain)
8. Short bench or carving stump
9. Cordless drill or screw driver
10. 3" deck or dry wall screws
11. 10" to 12" diameter log at least 20" long

Set your 10"–12" diameter log end up on your bench or carving stump. Screw it down with the 3" dry wall screws spaced around the base of the log. The screws will hold the log in place while it is being carved. Keep the working height of your carving in mind when you secure the log. If the log is too low, you will get a sore back; if it's too high your arms will get sorer than they need to be.

When everything is secure and you are completely dressed in the proper attire, you are ready to begin. The first cuts are relatively simple, but very important, so take your time and plan carefully. Follow the photos and don't be afraid to pre-mark your cuts with chalk. These are important steps for a beginner. By marking your cuts, you can concentrate on the basics of operating the chainsaw and not be distracted by deciphering a cut. Basically, the marks will help to train your eye. And chalk can be erased; saw cuts cannot.

As a chainsaw carver, I do not make patterns, per se. I do, however, use sketches quite often to plan out a sculpture. A preliminary sketch of the "Cub in a Stump" project helps me fix an image of the finished bear in my head. If you are a beginning carver, I suggest keeping a sketch or photo of the final piece nearby while you carve.

Blocking Out

1

With the log securely fastened to the work stump, you are ready to begin blocking out the carving.

2

The first cut determines the back of the head and the ears.

3

A second cut, angled in to meet the first, creates the angle for the backs of the ears.

4

This step marks, approximately, the fronts the ears. Make sure to leave enough wood to shape the ears later

5

A horizontal cut determines the top of the forehead. This cut is approximately 4" down from the top of the log and stops at the base of the cut made in Step 4.

6

Make sure the horizontal and vertical cuts are perfectly straight, making a 90° angle. the cut is not straight, the forehead will be tilted.

7 Divide the section for the ears in two. This should be the centerpoint of the log.

8 Start a 45° cut three inches from the center and take it down off the side of the log.

9 Follow the ear line straight down until you meet the edge of the cut made in Step 8. Do not overcut this step.

10 Repeat Steps 8 and 9 on the other side of the log.

11 Use a marker to draw in the ears. This will show you where to cut and help you to lay out the ears proportionally.

12 Make the cuts between the ears. Do not cut down into the bear's forehead.

13

Lay the bar flat on the forehead and push the tip of the chainsaw into the wood to remove the piece between the ears.

14

The results to this point. Be careful not to cut into the wood behind the ears. This will form the stump behind the bear.

15

Cut the top of the right ear...

16

...then the sides. You'll be making a cut down the outside of the ear and then in fro the bottom, as shown here

17

Cut the top and sides of the left ear in the same manner.

18

The ears are now completely blocked out.

19 Use a marker to draw on the next two cuts. These cuts will define the forehead and the nose.

20 A view of the top of the bear shows the cuts to this point and the positioning of the marks for the forehead and the nose.

21 Make the small cut for the forehead first. Notice the angle of this cut.

22 Remember to keep the bar horizontal as you make the slicing cut for the top of the nose.

23 When these cuts are made, you are ready to make the sides of the face.

24 Draw a guideline on the face as shown in this photograph.

25 Make a shallow cut to match the angle to the forehead.

26 Draw a line showing where to remove wood for the nose.

27 Begin the cut, being careful not to cut past the cut made in Step 25.

28 Finish the cut, again being careful not to c past the cut made in Step 25.

29 Cut the right side in the same manner.

30 The bear to this point. You can see the hea starting to appear from the wood.

31 Make a cut under the nose. This will define the bottom of the nose. Do not cut any deeper than the cheek.

32 The next cut begins where the top of the paws will be and meets the bottom of the cut made in Step 31.

33 Remove the piece of wood.

34 When the cut is complete it should look like a wedge of wood has been removed.

35 Start rounding the ears over to remove the square cuts.

36 Round both ears so that they are proportional.

37

Also trim the nose and bring it into proportion.

38

This is usually a two-step process, perhaps more.

39

The bear's face is now rounded and in proportion.

40

Remove the excess from the backs and the fronts of the ears. Tilt them a little so the appear to curve back.

41

Trim the nose back and bring it into proportion.

42

Define the sides of the head.

43 Clean up the area under the nose and head.

44 Now it's time to make the paws. Start by cutting a line down the center of the front of the log.

45 Next, cut a line to mark the bottoms of the paws.

46 Undercut the paws by cutting from the bottom of the log up to the line. Take wood off in small chunks.

47 Clean up around the paws; then round the paws over and knock off all of the square edges.

48 Define the paws with the tip of the chainsaw bar. The paws should be rounded and nicely shaped before moving on.

49

Move on to the head for more shaping and texturing. Use the side of the bar to make an indent for the eyebrows.

50

Use the side of the bar again to scoop out the eye sockets.

51

Round the top of the head by knocking off the sharp corners.

52

Trim behind the bear to create some space between the bear and the log behind it.

53

Cut in the nose. It looks like an upside down triangle. Then cut in nostrils on the left and right.

54

Make a horizontal cut for the mouth.

55 Scoop out the bottom of the jaw.

56 Cut around the bottom of the jaw so it looks like the bottom jaw fits into the top jaw.

57 Plunge back into the throat and cut the tongue.

58 The mouth should look like this when the plunge cut is complete.

Texturing

59 Now it's time to begin texturing. Start a groove between the bear's eyes. Remember you can shape and texture at the same time.

60 Continue the groove down the middle of the head. Begin texturing from here.

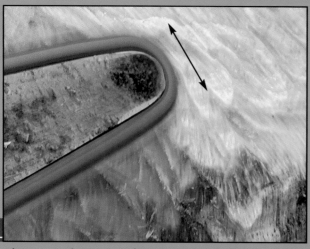

61

This is a close-up photograph of the texture. Move the tip of the bar up and down to create the hairlines.

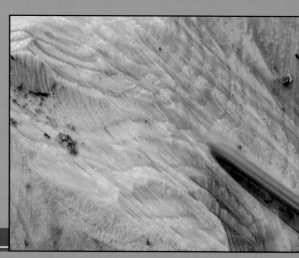

62

Pay attention to the direction of the hair flow. The texturing should follow the natural flow of the bear's hair.

63

Shape the inside of the ears using the side of the bar.

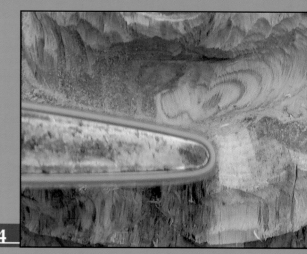

64

Texture the paws, making sure to cut with the grain of the wood.

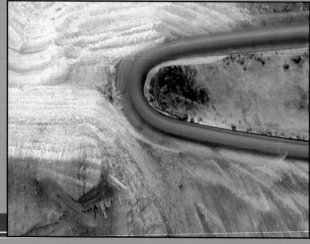

65

Cutting the eyes takes a steady hand. Control the speed of the saw and take your time.

66

Practice making eyes on a piece of scrapwood before making them on the bea Use only the tip of the bar.

When you are finished texturing, make a cut down the back of the log to control cracking.

The finished cub in a stump.

Chapter Four:
Carving a Caricature Bear

After carving the cub in a stump a few times, you are ready to move on to a more difficult project. A full size bear is the next step. The basics of blocking out and adding detail to the head remain the same, but you'll need to learn some new techniques for carving the body. You'll also need a little more equipment .

Before you start, you will need the following items:

1. Chaps
2. Safety glasses
3. Hearing protection
4. Steel-toed boots
5. Gloves
6. 14" diameter log about 4' tall
7. Chain saw (approx. 31cc to 55 cc) with a 12" carving bar
8. Chain saw (approx. 55cc) with an 18" standard bar

Start with the 18" standard bar. The first diagonal cut will determine the back of the head.

The second cut will determine the front of the ears.

Set the top of the forehead with a horizontal cut. Remember, at this point you are just blocking out the bear.

A second pass with the side of the bar level out the forehead.

Divide the top into two sections.

Make the side diagonal cut.

7 Make the vertical cut to remove the chuck of wood that will block out the right side of the face.

8 Make the same two cuts on the left side of the face.

9 Remove the wood between the ears by first making a cut along the inside of the left ear.

10 Make a second cut along the inside of the right ear.

11 Lay the bar flat against the forehead and make a plunge cut to free the wood between the ears.

12 The wood between the ears has been removed.

13

Cut the bottom of the ears. Be sure to leave enough material to shape the ears later.

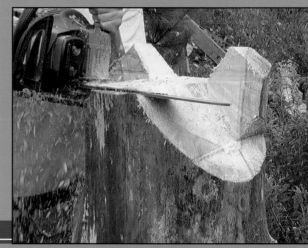

14

Divide the distance between the nose and the front of the ears and create the slope for the snout.

15

The cheek area is formed with two cuts, the first of which is a downward cut from the snout.

16

The second cut is made from the front of the snout and meets the first cut. Make the same two cuts to block out the cheek area on the opposite side of the face.

17

Start to block out the chin and the neck with a cut that angles down to the bottom of the cheek cut.

18

Make a vertical cut the width of the bar. This plunge cut will go all the way through the stump.

19

A horizontal cut that meets the bottom of the vertical cut finishes blocking in the neck and chin.

20

The bear looks like this when the block of wood from the neck is removed.

21

Clean up around the nose to bring it into proportion with the rest of the face.

22

Clean up the cuts around the cheeks and make crisper cuts in these areas.

23

Round any square corners and clean up around the ears.

24

Shape and round the back of the head.

25

Remove excess wood from the back of the ear on the left side.

26

Do the same on the right ear. Try to match the ears as closely as possible.

27

Start making the cuts that will take the excess off the bottom of the head.

28

The outline of the head is cut in with the chainsaw, but no excess wood has been removed yet.

29

Flatten the nose and angle it slightly it back into the neck.

30

Trim away the excess wood around the left side of the head that as outlined in Step 27

Make this same cut on the other side.

Shape the neck before moving on to the body.

Blocking Out the Body

This bear will be holding a sign, so the next step is to mark the bottom of the paws with a downward angled cut.

Approximately six inches approximately from the top of the paws, make an upward cut and take out a wedge.

Start the middle of the hourglass shape with a cut that curves from the inside of the cut out.

Cut back in at the bottom to form the bottom of the hourglass shape, approximately 18" down.

37

Cut straight in at the end of the cut.

38

This photo shows a front view of the cut.

39

The cut, from a side view, looks like this.

40

Take a shallow, concave cut to make the bear's back.

41

A deeper cut forms the hind quarters.

42

The finished cuts look like this.

43 Mark the under parts of the arms. The cut starts at the back and ends in the crease of the top wedge on the front.

44 Remove wood up to the cut; then do the same on the other side.

45 Cut down the side to make the leg.

46 Make a cut angled inward at the bottom to remove the chunk of wood.

47 Take a notch out of the back to define the rear end and back of the legs.

48 Draw on the sides of the belly with the tip of the saw.

49

Continue around the side of the bear…

50

…and down to the bottom part of the hourglass in the front.

51

Make the same cut on the opposite side.

52

The cuts should meet in the front like this.

53

Now cut up from the underside to meet the cut.

54

Follow the line all the way around the bea

55

Cut the knee and top of the foot deeper if needed.

56

Don't be afraid to make the cuts a little deeper.

57

Make the same cut on the other side.

58

Divide the knees and the top of the feet in two by cutting straight through the wood.

59

Then make two diagonal cuts in an X on top of the dividing line to separate the legs and form the crotch.

60

To remove the two pieces from the crotch area, lay the bar flat and cut through to the back. Remove one piece at a time.

61 One piece is removed in this photo. Repeat the flat cut to remove the second piece.

62 Round the knees into the crotch area.

63 The cuts should look like this at this point.

64 The bear is now completely blocked out. A side view shows the cuts to this point.

Adding Details

65 A front view of the blocked out bear. At this point, it's time to go back to the top and start putting in the detail.

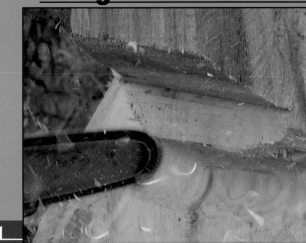

1 Define the neck by moving the tip of the b across the wood in a sweeping horizontal motion.

2 Clean up the face, making sure the cuts are straight and balanced from the right side to the left side

3 Clean up the nose also, bringing it more to the correct shape.

4 Bring the lower jaw into proportion and shape by removing a block of wood.

5 Using the tip of the bar, indent the forehead to separate the eyes.

6 Texture and shape the inside of the ears using the side of the tip of the bar.

7 Use the tip of the bar to carve out eye sockets

8 Round the front of the nose.

9 Clean up and smooth the side of the neck by using the side edge of the bar to remove small amounts of wood.

10 Draw in the line to show a tuft of hair around the neck. Start under the jaw on one side and bring it to the center under the chin.

11 Make the same cut on the other side. Don' make this cut too deep. About an inch will do.

12 Carefully remove wood up to the cut.

13 The tuft comes to a point under the chin.

14 Now you have a "round out" of the bear.

15 Switch to a 12" dime tip carving bar to carve the details. Use the tip of the bar to create a hollow in the bear's neck.

16 Shave off the wood at the tip of the bear's nose to remove the corner.

17 Use the tip of the bar to draw the v-shaped part of the nose.

18 Knock off the corners on the sides of the bear's nose.

19 Cut in the nostrils.

Caricature Bear

20 Round the side of the nose back into the face.

21 Starting at the back of the head and to the right of the crease down the center of the head, begin to carve the fur texture.

22 Use the tip of the bar to cut in short, shallow marks

23 Work down the side of the bear's cheek. The cuts in this area are close together.

24 Work back to the ear, making slightly larger and greater spaced cuts. A good photo of a bear will help you to make realistic fur.

25 Move down to the neck area. Notice that the cuts are staggered so that one cut starts near the middle of a previous cut, not at the end.

26

Make a vertical cut at the inside of the eye where the eye meets the snout.

27

Using the tip of the bar, outline the rest of the eye.

28

Remove a small amount of wood just below the outside corner of the eye. This will set the eye apart from the face.

29

Texture the eye area so that it blends smoothly into the face. The texture lines here are longer, shallower and closer and follow the contour of the eye.

30

Work the opposite side of the bear's face in the same manner.

31

A look at the bear straight on shows how the texturing gives the look of fur on the bear's face. Note that the eye on the left has not yet been outlined.

32

Outline the left eye with the tip of the bar.
Start at the inside corner and work your way
toward the outside corner. Refer to Steps
91-94.

33

Both eyes are roughed in.

34

Create the mouth with the tip of the bar.
This is just a quick, shallow cut straight into
the wood.

35

Widen and deepen the mouth by moving
the tip of the bar in a semi-circle.

36

With the tip of the bar, draw lines down the
side of the face to extend the mouth. Draw
these in first with a pencil if needed.

37

A line drawn under the mouth forms the tip
of a tongue inside the bear's mouth.

38 Turn the corners of the mouth down just a bit with shallow cuts using the tip of the bar.

39 Start to form the chin by making a sweeping cut that curves from left to right and leaves an indent under the mouth.

40 Use the tip of the saw to remove small amounts of wood and texture the area at the same time.

41 The bear to this point. Note how the texture falls on the face and the formation of the chin.

Shaping the Body

42 Switch back to the larger saw with the 18" standard bar to remove larger pieces or add large details. Begin to shape the paws by making sure that the cut above the paws is perfectly horizontal.

43 Make an angled downward cut to remove the top corner.

44

Make a smaller angled cut to shape the bottom of the paws.

45

Cut a trough behind the paws to separate them from the body of the bear.

46

Remove a triangular-shaped piece of wood from the left corner.

47

Remove a similarly shaped triangular chunk of wood from the right corner.

48

Cut straight in and make a vertical cut down the front of the bear's paws. Make a second shallower cut to the left of this line.

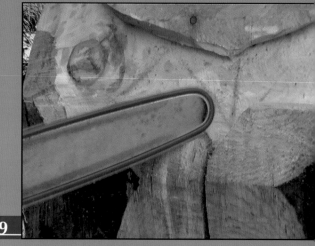

49

Remove a triangular shaped sliver of wood from the left side of the line.

50 Remove an similarly shaped piece of wood from the right side of the line.

51 Shape the bottom of the right paw by removing a slice of wood from the corner of the paw.

52 Do the same on the left side.

53 Shape up the area under the neck…

54 …and the area behind the paws before moving on. (You may be more comfortable using the smaller saw and dime tip bar in this area.)

55 Begin to add fur texture to the body of the bear with the tip of the chainsaw.

Move up toward the top of the bear, adding fur texture as you proceed.

Continue filling in texture on the bear's side.

Add fur texture to the area behind the bear's paws.

Round the sharp edges of the bear's paws, putting in some basic texturing as you go.

Add fur texture to the opposite side of the bear's body.

The back of the bear will be textured next.

Start near the top of the bear's back and work your way down his body.

As you work on the back, remove only small amounts of wood, as the back is basically the correct shape.

A small opening exists at the back of the bear sculpture from when you separated the feet. Clean up and shape that opening from the back.

Remove wood from the backs of the legs to shape them.

Smooth out the bottom of the piece with the side of the bar.

When the backs of the legs are shaped and textured to your satisfaction, move on to the front of the bear.

68

Continue adding texture until the body is completely covered in fur.

Shaping the Feet

69

Next, concentrate on shaping the feet. Remove a chuck of wood at the end of the foot to bring the foot back from the edge of the log.

70

Use the tip of the bar to remove wood from the top of the foot.

71

Round and shape the inside curve of the foot.

72

Remove wood from the area where the leg meets the body to form the crotch of the bear.

73

Remove wood from the outside of the bear leg.

4 Clean up the edge of the log all the way around the bear.

Z5 The textured bear is ready for his sign.

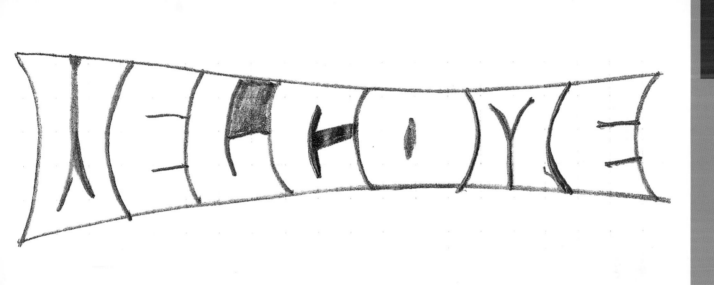

Carve the Sign

1 Temporarily secure the sign to the work stump.

2 With the tip of the dime tip carving bar, draw the lines for the rectangular area in which the word "Welcome" will be written.

Chainsaw Carving a Bear • 51

3

Draw the first strokes of each of the letters in the wood. You may want to outline these with a pencil first.

4

With the first strokes in place, you are ready to begin carving the letters. The letters will be reversed out of the sign.

5

Use the tip of the bar, slightly angled, to relieve the letters. Start with the "W."

6

Once the "W" is formed, move on to cut the crossbars out of the letter "E."

7

Next remove the wood from between the letter "L" and the letter "C."

8

Remove the wood from the center of the letter "C."

9

One cut creates the middle of the letter "O."

10

The center of the letter "M" is removed in a fashion similar to that of the letter "W" in Step 5.

11

Finish the word Welcome by cutting the crossbars for the final "E."

12

Raise the letters by cutting a deep trough around the outside of the letters.

13

Holding the bar flat against the sign, remove about half an inch of wood from the surface of the outside edges of the sign.

14

Make several cuts along the left and right edges of the board.

Place the sign behind the bear's paws and this welcome bear is finished.

Chapter Four:
Carving a Grizzly Bear

Now that you understand how to carve a cub in a stump and a standing caricature bear, it's time to work on a more complicated project. The process for carving a fierce grizzly starts out very similar to the other two projects in this book. You will use the same basic techniques to block in the face, with several changes to the shape of the face.

This bear will have its mouth open with its teeth showing. I will only show you how to carve the head here in this demonstration. Any number of body types can be added to this head. If you choose to carve a full bear, use a log about six feet tall. Follow the steps here to carve the head; then follow the blocking out techniques outlined in the standing caricature bear project, using reference material to alter the pose to create a more lifelike grizzly. Working on a larger bear may require the use of scaffolding. Be sure to follow all safety precautions to the letter.

To carve the grizzly bear in this demonstration, you'll need:

1.	Chaps
2.	Safety glasses
3.	Hearing protection
4.	Steel-toed boots
5.	Gloves
6.	Chainsaw (approximately 31 cc to 55 cc) with a 14"–16" bar with 3/8 low profile chain
7.	Chainsaw (approximately 31 cc to 55 cc) with a 12" carving bar
8.	4' log approximately 14" in diameter

1 Start with the 14"–16" bar with a 3/8 low profile chains. Cut the top of the log at a slight angle.

2 Follow the same blocking-out techniques as those used for the standing bear. First, cut than angled piece of wood from the back o the log. This will be the back of the ears.

3 Make a vertical cut for the front of the ears. Note how deep this cut is as compared to the previous cut.

4 Then make the horizontal cut for the forehead and the top of the head.

5 Make sure this cut is flat and follows the same slight angle as made in Step 1.

6 Divide this portion of the log into two eve parts. These parts will form the ears.

7 Make an angled cut on the right side to start the face.

8 Make the same cut on the opposite side.

9 Then, make a cut along the ears to remove the pieces.

10 Knock the corners off both ears.

11 Block out the top of this ear.

12 Make the same cut on the other ear.

13 Lay the saw bar flat against the head and remove the wood between the ears.

14 Block out the bottom of both ears.

15 Then make a second cut to remove the excess wood.

16 Set the forehead and nose by making another slightly angled cut across the top of the bear.

17 Make a shallow cut down the side of the face to start the cheek.

18 Remove a piece of wood with a slicing cut. Do both sides, keeping them even.

19 Trim the nose. It needs to be slim.

20 Continue to clean up around the nose. Notice that I haven't yet cut under the muzzle, like I did on the other bears.

21 Start on the back of the head to make sure you have the ears in the right spot.

22 Cut the excess off the fronts of both ears.

23 Then trim the backs of the ears. Keep both sides even.

24 Round the head.

25 Start to round the face, but don't cut under the neck yet.

26 Cut the other side.

27 Remove the excess below the cut. Do this on both sides.

28 Clean up the side of the mouth. Notice the mouth still runs to the neck.

29 Now it's time to define the bottom of the muzzle. Angle this cut up from the neck to where the bottom of the mouth will be.

30 Draw the outline of an open mouth on the face of the bear. These lines show how far open you want the mouth to be.

31 Then all you have to do is follow the lines. Switch to a 12" carving bar for the remaining steps.

32 Run the bar along the mouth, removing only the width of the bar inside the lines. Do both sides.

33 Remove the same amount of wood from the front of the mouth.

34 Define the area under the mouth and chin.

35 Then go back and clean up the edge all the way around the mouth.

36 Now to make the teeth. Cut up from the bottom lip at an angle.

37 For the bottom teeth, make a plunge cut from the side at an angle.

38 Then plunge cut from the front to the back of the mouth. This will create a stop cut when you need to remove the waste from the side.

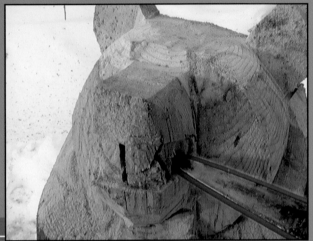

39 Use plunge cuts to remove the waste from the side. You should feel when you hit the stop cut. Remove the chunk of wood after you've cut all the way around the piece.

40 Then do the same on the other side.

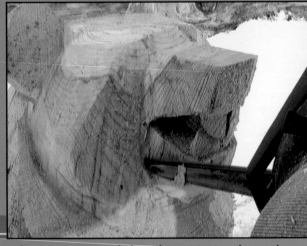

41 Clean up around the chin. Notice how the teeth are now blocked in.

42 Drag the bar around the bottom of the mouth to blend it into the neck.

43

A view from the front shows the same cuts under the chin.

44

Now go back to the top of the head and work your way down, detailing even more as you go.

45

Round the ears more…

46

… and shape the insides.

47

Cut around the back of the ears and start adding hair.

48

Use the tip of the bar to shape the bridge between the eyes.

49

Start at the top of the face…

50

… and work your way down around the neck.

51

Here's the same cut on the opposite side. Start at the top of the face…

52

… and continue down around the neck.

53

Now start to shape the nose.

54

Round and smooth the nose, going around this area again and again, until you like the way it looks.

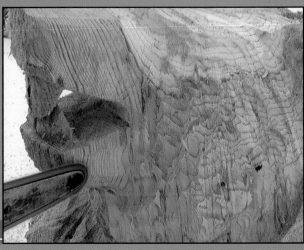

55 Next, move to the chin. Round the area until you are satisfied with the result.

56 Take more wood out from under the chin to make a lip.

57 Now, start on the teeth, thinning them out from the center first. Remove very little wood at a time, and go slowly.

58 Carefully point the teeth.

59 Then round each to resemble the shape of a tooth.

60 Once you have the front of the teeth shaped, then it is time to shape the teeth from the back. This step takes a lot of patience.

61

Define the tongue from the side.

62

Then define the lip and the tongue from the front.

63

Here is another view of the front of the tongue being shaped.

64

Go back and define the nose.

65

Flare out the top lip by removing some wood between the nose and the lip.

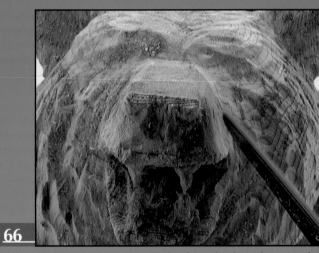

66

When you are satisfied with the shape of t nose, cut the nostrils.

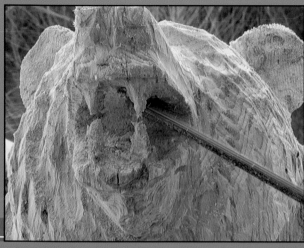

67 The top of the mouth needs a little clean-up work. Be careful—the teeth come out easier than they went in.

68 Blend the bottom of the jaw into the neck. Continue blending and adding texture in this area until you are satisfied with the result.

69 Cut away wood to form the tuft of hair under the bear's neck.

70 Carve the left and right eyes. (If you need additional instructions on cutting eyes, refer to the previous two projects.)

The face of a fierce grizzly is finished. If you are working on a full grizzly, continue blocking out and adding texture to the body. You can follow the blocking-out steps for the standing caricature bear. Be sure to use your reference material to put the bear in a more lifelike stance for a grizzly. Any number of body types can be added to this head.

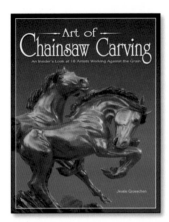

Art of Chainsaw Carving
ISBN: 978-1-56523-250-1 **$19.95**

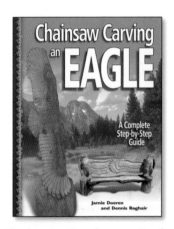

Chainsaw Carving an Eagle
ISBN: 978-1-56523-253-2 **$16.95**

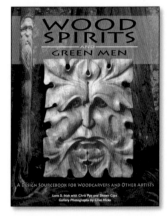

Wood Spirits and Green Men
ISBN: 978-1-56523-261-7 **$19.95**

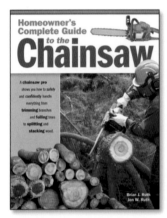

**Homeowner's Complete
Guide to the Chainsaw**
ISBN: 978-1-56523-356-0 **$24.95**

The Little Book of Whittling
ISBN: 978-1-56523-274-7 **$12.95**

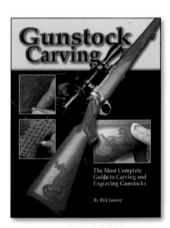

Gunstock Carving
ISBN: 978-1-56523-166-5 **$19.95**

WOODCARVING
ILLUSTRATED

ScrollSaw
woodworking
& CRAFTS

In addition to being a leading source of woodworking books and
DVDs, Fox Chapel also publishes two premiere magazines. Released
quarterly, each delivers premium projects, expert tips and techniques
from today's finest woodworking artists, and in-depth information
about the latest tools, equipment, and materials.

Subscribe Today!
Woodcarving Illustrated: **888-506-6630**
Scroll Saw Woodworking & Crafts: **888-840-8590**
www.FoxChapelPublishing.com